Living a Second Chance

Fredrick Sipe

Living a Second Chance

Library of Congress Control Number:		2017938391
ISBN-13:	Paperback:	978-1-64045-195-7
	PDF:	978-1-64045-196-4
	ePub:	978-1-64045-197-1
	Kindle:	978-1-64045-198-8

Printed in the United States of America

LitFire LLC
1-800-511-9787
www.litfirepublishing.com
order@litfirepublishing.com

CONTENTS

CHAPTER ONE

THE BEGINNING

Hello, my name is Fredrick Sipe. I was born on April 16, 1976 in Charlottesville, Virginia. My friends and family call me Bubba. I would like to tell you a little about my life and the accident that I suffered in 1997. I have three sisters and three brothers. My brother Lee, my two sisters Minnie and Mary, and I have the same mother but different fathers. My other siblings, two brothers and a sister, have the same father, Aubrey Fredrick Sipe. Their mother's name was Ruby.

Lee, Minnie, and Mary were all born out of my mother's marriage to Richard Morningwake. A couple of years later, Richard and my mother separated. Then Pauline, my mother, met my father, who as I have indicated already had children of his own. About a year later, I was born. For a time everything went well. Then my dad started drinking heavily and his behavior began to get out of control. My mother left him when I was about three years old, and moved with us to Pennsylvania because she has a lot of family there.

My Aunt Martha and Uncle Larry Klinger had two kids of their own, Larry and Eddie Klinger. They were older than all of us, especially me. I was the baby. We were all very close, so they let us stay with them for a few weeks until my mother found us a place of our own, in the city of Harrisburg. It wasn't much, we didn't have a lot of money, but love kept us together.

As I grew older I made a lot of friends. One of them, a boy named George Radabough, was like another brother to me. We did everything together. Even in school we took the same classes, so we were rarely apart. We got into a few fights with other kids, both in and out of school. I know fighting isn't the answer to everything, but you had to fight back or you would get picked on every day!

When I was about twelve I made another friend, a boy named Guy, Jr. His dad, Guy, Sr., had his own tree-trimming business, and let me work for him. It was good because it kept me out of trouble and put money in my pocket. Guy, Sr. was a good man. His wife Sue was also nice to me; she always made sure we had enough to eat, both before and after work, and I stayed at her house on some nights and weekends.

My brother's friend Jimmy and I had some things in common. We both liked dogs, so we would walk ours and talk about him and my brother when they were younger. He told me about things they had done similar to what George, and Guy, and I did in our free time. Jimmy's sister Michelle had a boyfriend whose name was Macho. He was cool, and almost everyone knew him. He taught me a lot about the streets and the game of handball. It's something like racquetball except you don't use a racket, you use your hands. The wall we used was on the side of a warehouse where all the young people hung out. Handball was popular with everyone; even my brother tried to play. That was really funny to watch, because he would go to hit the ball and would miss it entirely.

My teenage years went by. When I turned sixteen I dropped out of school and got a job in a vegetable factory. About that time, my family moved away from Harrisburg and into the country. My brothers and sisters and I all had a lot of fun there, we rode dirt bikes and swam and hung out at the nearby creek, but only on the weekends because we worked a lot during the week. Some close friends from Harrisburg also moved out near us: Sharon and Don and their kids, Mojo, Timmy, Lindy, and their young brothers Donny and Jeremy. I loved hanging out at their place; we would play horseshoes and shoot guns, and had a lot of fun together. Several members of my family worked with me at the vegetable factory.

After I had been working there for a couple of months, I met the love of my life, a girl named Tasha

Leigh Bailey. It was love at first sight. But before we started dating, we both joked around a lot at work and got to know each other. She was with another guy at the time, but it was clear from what she had told me that they were not getting along.

One weekend, we hooked up and went to a party at my cousin's house, and that's where it all started. Eventually we moved in together with my mother and family.

Me, Tasha, my mom and her ex-boyfriend, Mike.

Tasha already had a son, Brandon, who was two years old. Her mother and the rest of her family did not like the idea of me and Tasha getting together, so it was kind of an ugly start at first. Her ex-boyfriend took Brandon with him when they separated, a separation which was very hard on Tasha, and for which I felt somewhat responsible. I hated to see her go through that pain. I just kept telling her things would work out. Soon enough she had gotten comfortably settled in with my family and everyone grew very close to her.

About three months later, Tasha became pregnant with our first child. It was a boy! We named him Mardey Dalton Sipe. Having a child can change you to make you a better person in life. I left the factory and took a new job in construction doing basement waterproofing, which paid more money. My friend Jimmy helped me get the job and worked with me. It was very hard work. My brother Lee eventually worked with us too. The three of us worked our asses off but found ways to make the job fun as well.

This is me, Tasha, and our son Mardey Dalton Sipe on his first Christmas before the accident.

Tasha and I eventually moved into an apartment nearby where my friend Jimmy had lived. By this time Jimmy and I had become very close; he and his wife Ronda and their three daughters, Chris, Al, and Boog (a nickname we all called her), would ride horses and go fishing with me and Tasha.

Jimmy and I did a lot of other things together, just the two of us, including the job he had helped me get in the construction business. Being young, it was hard for me and Tasha to keep up with everyday life and the costs of living. Tasha took a job as a waitress, and was eventually promoted to bartender. That helped out a lot. With her working as a bartender and me as a waterproofer, we were both making decent money.

Later that year, we were thrilled to discover that Tasha was pregnant again. This time it was a girl! We named her Chelsey Leigh Sipe. She was a very beautiful little girl. We thought that we now had the perfect family, even though we struggled at times and never owned a house of our own. All that mattered to us was that we had each other.

This is me and Tasha visiting a friend at the hospital after giving birth.

Around this time, something good happened between Tasha and her mother – they started talking again. As their relationship improved, Tasha began to visit her mom and also began to see her other son, Brandon, again. Soon enough, Brandon began staying at our house on the weekends. I grew to know the kid pretty well; I would take him with me and my kids fishing and doing other fun things. He was a great kid, and I would have done anything for him.

After some time, I even started going to my mother-in-law's house for holidays. I sensed that her family never liked me too much, but I still tried for the sake of Tasha and Brandon. One Christmas Eve, her mom threw a party. Her brother was there, and we never did get along. After drinking some beer, we got into an argument, so I just left and went home. I didn't want to cause any trouble for Tasha or Brandon, so I stopped visiting my mother-in-law's house. I just did not want any more arguing or fighting. Staying away was the best thing to do.

When I turned twenty-one, Tasha and I went out to celebrate my birthday at a bar. After a while, we left the bar and went to my friend Jimmy's house. After hanging out for a few hours, we decided to leave, and began heading home on my motorcycle, but on the way we were forced off the road by another vehicle. I could not control the bike, I did everything I could, but we still ended up hitting a guard rail. We flipped into a gully that was about twenty feet deep.

All I can remember is flying into a tree; we crashed out in the middle of nowhere. But thank God, somehow a farmer saw the light and heard the bike's engine running. He came rushing over to us and knew right away that we were in terrible shape. So he called 911 and Lifeline rushed us to Hershey Medical Center. The doctors immediately leaped into action, doing everything they could to help us. I had broken my neck very badly-my third, fourth, and fifth vertebrae. They had to put a halo on my head to keep my neck stable, so that I would not cause any more damage. From what my family told me, I learned that Tasha was also in very bad shape. I don't think she ever woke up; she was on life support; it was a nightmare.

The doctors needed to operate on me right away, but before they started, my family told them to take me into Tasha's room to see her. I don't remember any of it, but my family told me later that I had done nothing but cry and blame myself when I saw her lying motionless in the hospital bed. After the operation, I went into a deep coma. My family stood by my side the whole time; my mother never left the hospital. My Aunt Josie and Uncle Bobby Dove and their kids Scottie, Donna, and Deb, tried to get my mother to go out and get something to eat, but she wouldn't listen.

As for Tasha's family, the doctors told them there was nothing they could do. So her parents had a horrible decision to make: either to keep her on life support or to let her go. I don't know which choice they made, but I do know that it was very hard on both my family and hers. A simple birthday celebration had turned into a real mess for everyone. Tasha's family blamed me for everything, which I do understand. To this day I still blame myself.

Despite all of the tragedy and pain our families went through together, Tasha's family didn't want anyone from mine to see Tasha. They wouldn't even let them go to the funeral. But before the doctors took Tasha off life support, my sisters Minnie and Mary snuck into her room and talked to her. They talked about me and the kids, and as they did, they saw a tear running down her cheek. It was very upsetting. My sisters knew that Tasha understood what was going on. As for the funeral, both Minnie and Mary went, despite being forbidden from attending. As this was going on, Tasha's mother tried to take my kids away from me. But my mother and the rest of my family would not let that happen. Aunt Josie and her family helped my mother get a lawyer and fight for custody.

This is my mom with my two kids Chelsey and Mardey Sipe when they were babies.

The court battle lasted a couple of months, but in the end the judge awarded custody to my mother. I was glad of the result when I learned of what had happened, but I wish it had not gone down that way between our families.

As for me, I was in a coma for a couple of months. Hershey Medical could not keep me any longer, so they sent me to West Shore Health and Rehabilitation Center, an assisted living facility. I didn't know what was going on, but I could feel my family with me. I dreamed a lot, and I felt something wasn't right with Tasha. I started to wake up slowly from my coma, becoming progressively more aware of what had happened to me. I remember that my friend George and his brother Jake were always there talking to me; even though I was still only half-awake, I was able to see them before drifting back to sleep. Once my friends had left, the nurses came into my room to take care of me, and as they were doing so, I woke up enough to see what was happening. When I saw that they were changing my diaper as if I were a little baby, all I could say to myself was, *What the hell, I can't believe this shit.*

When I woke up fully, I found myself on a respirator, with a tracheostomy tube to help me breathe. My family came to see me, but I couldn't speak, couldn't ask questions, and I kept wondering why no one had mentioned Tasha. I came to believe that one of my nightmares had come true-she was gone.

My family didn't want to tell me about her death because they thought the news would set me back in my recovery. Finally, I realized what had happened to Tasha from the way in which they kept avoiding the subject. They had guessed right; learning of her death made me want to give up. Suddenly all the pain of being on life support and not being able to move meant nothing to me.

I was heartbroken, realizing I would never walk again or be able to do things I had once done, such as holding Tasha in my arms. It just made me want to give up. But my family kept reassuring me about my kids, and all I could think about was what Tasha would have wanted me to do, and that would be to keep fighting and to raise the kids well. So I started to do everything that I could to get better, and with the help of a therapist I was able to get off life support and regain the ability to breathe on my own.

CHAPTER TWO

THE ROAD TO RECOVERY

Once I could breathe on my own, I had to learn how to eat and swallow again. After a week or so, with the help of a therapist I was able to eat and swallow. But the doctors wanted to make sure that I could digest my food, so they put me on a big machine that monitored my digestive system. They fed me some terrible stuff – I could not even begin to tell you what it tasted like or to guess what it was – to see if I could swallow without choking. The tests went well. Finally I was able to eat without suffering from the smell of food being delivered to other patients.

My first good meal since the accident was a Big Mac, chicken nuggets, and French fries. I had been dreaming about that exact meal while I was asleep. Let me tell you, it was delicious!

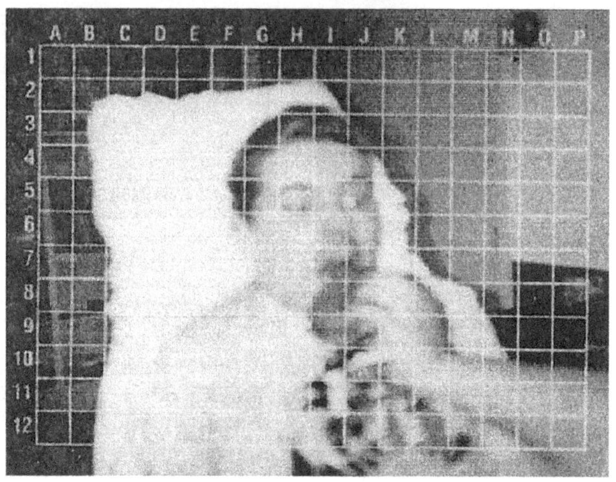

This is me eating my first BigMac Meal in the nursing home after all the testings.

My next goal was to get into a wheelchair. It required a lot of therapy, pain, and time, but it was worth it – I finally reached the point where I could get into a wheelchair. I even started to feel a little better about myself. One thing bothered me a lot, however, and that was the fact that my friend Jimmy, with whom I was so close, never came to see me. I loved the dude like family, and his absence broke my heart.

After some time, I was able to go home for a visit. It was the week before Christmas, so my family celebrated the holiday early. The nursing home planned transportation for me, and we were grateful to them for giving us a chance to be together. It felt great to be with my family over the holidays and away from the nursing home. That was something I had thought I would never be able to do again. On Christmas Day, when it was time to open presents, my kids, nephews, and nieces brought my gifts to me one at a time, and I tore off the wrapping paper with my teeth. It was very funny and they all loved it.

This picture is my mom holding my present for me to open on my first visit home from the nursing home.

The following day the van from West Shore Health & Rehab came to pick me up, and as I was being loaded in, my sister Minnie and my mom started to cry. I asked why, and they told me that I had to go to court about the accident. My heart dropped. After having such a good time with my family, I received this bad news. I told them it would be okay and everything would work out. But although I didn't want my family to know it, deep inside I was scared.

A few days later, we went to the court hearing. As I was pushed into the courtroom, I felt embarrassed to be seen by so many people, because I was so weak that I could barely hold my head up. I still had the trache in my neck and couldn't even speak well enough for the judge to understand me. The lawyer translated for me, but in the end the judge waived the hearing. We were told to come back in a month so the court could decide what to charge me with.

When I went back, they put me in a private room and charged me with vehicular manslaughter. I assume it was because they didn't have any evidence of us getting run off the road. I was told that if I ever walked again I could spend five to ten years in prison. None of that mattered to me; I would have done anything to take Tasha's place. She had been my life, and I loved her. As we left the courtroom, I told my mother and sisters everything would work out. The judge had given us sobering news, but for me and my family that part of my ordeal was over.

A few months later, at my therapist's request, a wheelchair company came to the nursing home to fit me for a power chair. It was pretty exciting! After they took my measurements for the chair, they lent me one to practice in until my family could purchase one for me. It took some time and a lot of crashes to get used to it. But when I did learn how to drive it, it gave me some freedom and confidence.

Minnie came in every week to make me a grocery list. I had a lot of food stashed in the nurses' refrigerator and a lot more hidden in my dressers. It was all candy, cereal, and chips. I could not stand the food they served; it tasted horrible! So I had Minnie buy junk food for me. The nurses would even come in to keep me company and to munch on my snacks. They all loved me, except when my nieces and nephews, Paul, Rita, Brandy, and Randy, and my two kids came to visit. They all raised a lot of hell! Some of the nurses would laugh at them, and others would complain. But I didn't care. They knew that I was only trying to live a normal life.

That's very hard to do in a nursing home. I did show respect to everyone, especially the elderly. By now, because of all the love my kids and family had for me, I wanted to keep my confidence up and keep fighting. Even though I was paralyzed, I started to realize that I could live with my disability.

In the nursing home I had a good friend named Buzz. He was really cool and down to earth, someone I could relate to. Buzz had been in a car accident resulting in the loss of his legs, and that had left him confined to a wheelchair. He had already been in the nursing home for quite some time when I arrived, so he could drive his power chair very well. Buzz and I became close, and we were fortunate to have the privilege to drink a couple of beers at night, with the doctor's approval of course. I could not move my arms or hands, so Buzz would sit beside me and give me a drink when I wanted one, which I thought was funny, though I appreciated it. Monday nights we would watch football and have our beer. I am glad I met him, because he made the stay at the nursing home bearable.

This is me and Buzz in the nursing home.

I had to do therapy every day. The therapists did everything they could to help me regain more movement and feeling in my body. I did regain some feeling in my shoulders, but it wasn't much. We worked on making them stronger and on strengthening my neck as well.

Within a couple of months, I felt myself getting better, and I began to have more feeling and movement in my arms. I could even move my right arm in and out. It wasn't much, but this improvement gave me enough hope and confidence to keep fighting. My family was proud of how much I was accomplishing, but I could see in their eyes the sorrow and pain at the fact that I would never be able to walk again. The whole family took it very hard.

My brother Lee took it especially hard, because before the accident we had been very close. We had taken to hanging out almost every day, and, as I have said, we worked together with my friend Jimmy. After work we would go out to drink and play some pool at a local bar, and if anyone tried to mess with my brother I would not give him a chance to defend himself; I would tell him to sit down and that I would take care of it, and I always did just that.

My mom, Minnie, and Mert also found it very hard to accept my condition. I guess my friends did as well, because the only friends who came to see me in the nursing home were Jake, George, and Guy.

Guy brought his dad along, and their visits meant a lot to me.

This is me and George Radabaugh when he visited me in the nursing home.

I need to tell you some other embarrassing things I had to deal with. I had to learn to use the bathroom with the help of nurses, which was hard for me to accept. Later, my mother and sister had to learn how to help me do this, along with everything else necessary to caring for me. I was more comfortable with having my family help me use the bathroom than anyone else. To learn about how to help me, as well as my various options for relieving myself, my mother and I had to meet a urologist whose name was Dr. Owens. To this day, he is the coolest doctor

I have ever met. We had to go to the hospital to meet him, and I had to stay overnight. My mother was going to stay there with me, but Dr. Owens said he would call her a cab. I laughed and said it would be way too much money. So he said he would just take her home. I was shocked, I thought to myself, *What doctor would do that?* Dr. Owens explained everything to us about going to the restroom. I had the option to get a catheter in my bladder or to continue what I had been using in the nursing home, which was painful and time-consuming. So I chose to get the catheter.

After that was done, my family had to set up home health care, which involved purchasing and installing equipment such as a lift, a bed, and other things I needed to carry on everyday living. The only thing I could not get in the nursing home was my power chair, because of a lot of red tape from the insurance company, which refused to pay for one until I went home. The power chair I had in the nursing home was a loaner, so the staff gave me a regular push chair to take home.

CHAPTER THREE

COMING HOME

Before I was able to go home, my mother and family had to find us a place to live where the doors were wide enough for my chair to fit through. They found a place back in the city of Harrisburg. It wasn't the best place, but it was enough for them to bring me home. When it was time for me to leave the nursing home, Buzz and all of the staff threw a going-away party for me. A lot of them were sad to see me go, because I kept everyone laughing, even the elderly. I knew I would miss them too, but there was nothing better than going home; I had dreamed about that day since waking up from my coma.

It took some time for me to get used to everything in the new house, but it was good to be home with my mother and my kids. It felt good to wake up in the morning to my family. My mother had coffee ready for me every morning, which doesn't sound like much, but after what I had been through it meant a lot.

After waking up, we would all eat breakfast together in my room, because the nurse did not come until nine a.m. After eating, it was time for my kids to get ready to go to school. That first morning, I met my home health care nurse for the first time. I had to get used to another person helping me – brushing my teeth, giving me a bath, and more. I felt very uncomfortable, but I had to live with it. After my bath, the nurse and my mother had to get me up in my chair for the first time at home. It was difficult at first, but we managed to do it, and now it only takes minutes. Around eleven a.m., I had to go to therapy. The transportation company had to come and pick me up, then take me where I needed to go. My family had not yet installed a permanent wheelchair ramp for me to get outside, but we did have two portable metal ramps to use in the meantime. Before they would pick me up I had to be outside waiting for them. They didn't care if it was raining, snowing, hailing, or anything else; the van still came to pick me up and deliver me to therapy. But it was the only transportation I had at the time. The entire process of getting loaded into the van was kind of scary. I had to position myself on the retractable wheelchair ramp that lifted me up into the van. Then they had to strap me down so that I would remain stable during the drive. When we arrived for therapy, the therapist evaluated my sensitivity by poking me with pins, to see what I could feel. She wasn't being cruel; she poked just hard enough for me to feel it. She also tested me by putting either hot or cold bags on my skin.

After the evaluation, the therapist was done with me. She was very rude! She told me that I would never regain more movement or feeling! That really disappointed me, because in my heart I felt the opposite of what she said. Besides, I think that therapists should be encouraging and not so negative with their patients. Especially with someone who is new to his disability. So the physicians decided they could not do therapy on me anymore. I guess it was for insurance reasons. Later I found out that if a patient does not show improvement within a month, that patient's insurance will not continue to pay for therapy.

When I returned home, all I could think about was the therapist telling me that I would never be able to move again. I was determined to prove her wrong. *After all,* I thought, *I have already beaten the odds.* After the accident, everyone thought I would never breathe, eat, or do anything on my own ever again. But I am still here and fighting my disability.

Something else that gave me confidence was listening to Christopher Reeve, the actor who famously portrayed Superman in *Superman: The Movie* and its sequels. I saw him on TV a lot and also listened to his audio book. He had been through a lot himself, having become a quadriplegic due to a horseback riding accident, and he was someone I could relate to. I became very happy when he mentioned stem cells, which are embryo cells that could be injected into our spines to produce new nerves and hopefully let us walk again. So I just wanted to keep myself healthy until the use of embryonic stem cells was approved by the government.

A couple of years later, however, it was announced on the evening news that Christopher Reeve had died. I was very sad to hear about his passing, and was touched by what his son said when the news people interviewed him. Reeve's son had done for him everything my kids do for me. But I couldn't believe what the reporters asked his wife. They asked, "How are you going to say goodbye?" Dana responded, "I had eight years to say goodbye." I liked her response, though it was very sad. But I know Chris would have wanted every disabled person to live his or her life and to keep on fighting for the cause.

After my insurance refused to pay for therapy anymore, I learned of United Cerebral Palsy (UCP), an organization that helps children and adults with disabilities, including cerebral palsy. UCP has different programs that you can get into if you are disabled, and trust me, you need all the help you can get. They helped me to get home therapy, and every day I worked hard in those therapy sessions. I started to get some feeling and movement back. It wasn't a lot, but we kept working with my shoulders because they were one of the strongest parts of my body.

After a few months, I was able to bend my forearms in and out on a table. I thought it was pretty exciting. Then my other therapist, who worked on my legs, got me a stander through UCP. It took some time, but eventually I was able to stand up in it. It felt so great to be able to stand again. George Warner was one of my favorite therapists.

As time passed, I kept working on my upper body and my legs, the muscles I needed for the stander. I was not yet able to feed myself, but that was one of my long-term goals. My most immediate goal was to get a power chair and a wheelchair ramp so that I could access the outdoors on my own. I finally got approved for my chair! I was so excited!

But now I had to undergo another evaluation. This time it was for a good reason – they just needed to measure me and fit me for my chair. The evaluation took longer than we had expected, and my sister Minnie, my nurse, and I had to rush down the elevators to where the transportation vans were, but we were a few minutes late, so they left. I could not believe they had just left us there. You would think they would have waited for us. We did not know what to do, but luckily, Hershey Medical gave us a ride home. When we arrived, believe it or not, we found that my chair had gotten home before we did. After all of the complaining, it was worth it.

I could not go outside at first because I still didn't have a ramp, but that was fine because I needed to practice in my power chair. A couple of weeks later, UCP found a company to build me a ramp. Now that was awesome! It only took them a week to finish it. It was nice and wide! So now I could go outside whenever I wanted to, though of course someone had to open the door for me, but I didn't mind that small inconvenience.

A few months later, Minnie and Sam got married! Then Sam started to change. It was as if he didn't want to be bothered by anyone, not even Dave! Now that was a shock, because Dave and Sam had been friends for a very long time. At the time, I chalked Sam's strange behavior up to new love. Even without Sam, Dave and I continued to hang out a lot. We got pretty close. He played around with my kids. Then one day, he told me he was going to get married. I was happy for him, and I still wish I could have gone to the wedding. But I could not go because it would have been necessary to climb a lot of steps to get into the building. Dave wanted Sam to be his best man, and Sam agreed to do so. But on the wedding day, Sam let Dave down – he didn't show up. I could see it hurt Dave, and he stopped talking to Sam.

Sam continued to act strangely. He and my brother Lee even got into a fight. That ended our friendship too. Dave and I were still hanging out together; it was as if I had known him forever. He and I talked about everything. One day, Dave told me that his wife had gotten pregnant but that he didn't want anyone to know. He and his wife were waiting to make sure that nothing went wrong with the pregnancy before telling everyone the good news, so I promised to keep the secret. I didn't tell anyone, not even my mother. A few months later, Dave told my mom, and we were all happy for him and his wife. He and I were always joking around; he made fun of me because of the way I dealt with my kids, always giving in to their demands. I told him, "You just wait until you have your kid, and you will feel my pain." We would both just laugh.

I didn't want my kids to grow up in Harrisburg. I wanted to move. But then something else happened to me. I got a bed sore and ended up in the hospital. I had surgery for it and soon recovered and went home. The physicians ordered a bed with an air mattress for me so that I would not get any more sores. I was doing well, but then a year later I caught pneumonia and ended up back in the hospital. They admitted me to stay so that I could get some medicine through an IV. My mother and I told the doctors that I needed to be on an air mattress, and they said they would take care of it, but they never did. After a week or so, when

I was much better and they had discharged me, they found a bed sore on my bottom. I thought to myself, *Not again,* because I had gone through hell with the last one. So I was very upset, and when I got home I called a lawyer and told him what had happened. He decided to take my case, and we sued the hospital. After a few months they finally gave me an offer for a settlement and I accepted it.

CHAPTER FOUR

TRAGEDY STRIKES AGAIN

One day in the year 2000, I was getting my bath like I do every morning, when suddenly my sister Minnie came running into the house, and told us a kid had just been hit by a car out on the main road. Concerned for my son, she asked me, "Where is Dalton?" We thought for sure he was upstairs in his room watching TV. But when my mom went upstairs to check his room, he wasn't there. All of our hearts dropped to the floor. Minnie and Mom ran out to the main road to see if it was him, and, sad to say, it was. Eyewitnesses said he had been trying to beat the traffic on his bike. A car was coming toward him and I guess the driver thought that Dalton would make it onto the curb, but his foot slipped and he didn't make it. The car hit him so hard that he flew up and hit the windshield and cracked it.

After hitting the windshield, he fell back onto the road, and luckily a neighbor went running over to him. Dalton was not breathing, so the man began to give him CPR. I thank God that he was there. Just then, Lifeline landed. They rushed Dalton to the hospital-the same one where his mother and I had been taken years before. Deb, my Aunt Josie's daughter, worked there, and having seen me and Tasha brought in, and now seeing my son injured, was very heartbreaking for her.

Dalton was in bad shape. The surgeons had to operate to relieve some fluid from his head. He slipped into a coma, and breathing tubes were placed in his nose. It was very hard to see him lying there. One nurse picked him up and put him on my lap. I tried to speak to him through my tears; it was very hard on me and my family. A week later, after going through hell again, my son woke up. But he was not himself – he thought my sister was his mom; he seemed like a little baby. He had to learn how to walk and talk again. My family and I were there by his side through it all. He didn't want to cooperate with the doctors and therapists, so I would go in almost every day and try to work with him. Even though it tore me up inside seeing him like that, I had to be strong for him. I was like his coach. I encouraged him to concentrate and work on what the therapists wanted him to do. Every day he showed more and more improvement.

When Dalton had gotten better after doing a lot of therapy, we were finally allowed to bring him home. He was not the same boy, but my son was finally home with the family. My daughter, Chelsey, was very upset by the accident, but she is a very strong girl. I explained everything about her brother and I told her she had to try to get along with him and ignore some things he would do. So she did. Chelsey is a very smart girl, and she reminds me very much of her mother. About a year later, my son was doing a lot better; he was getting a lot of his memory and personality back. I am so proud of him and Chelsey. One thing that did change a lot was his temperament; he had to take medication to control his emotions, particularly anger. But the doctor kept switching the medication he had to take. I think that is why he began having so much trouble with his anger and so many problems in school. But eventually it all got resolved.

CHAPTER FIVE

THE MOVE

Finally my family and I were able to move into our new home. It was great! It was out of the city, in a quiet neighborhood where my kids could be safe, and it was zoned for a good school. As for myself, I could finally enjoy a shower instead of taking a birdbath every day. And everything was wheelchair-accessible so that I could get around. I even had a ramp to get in and out of the house. The doors and everything else were nice and wide. I could fly around, and have a lot of fun with the kids in my chair!

This is me, uncle bobby, and Aunt Josie Dove visiting me at my new house.

But none of this would have been possible if it wasn't for a great lady named Reba. She helped me with all of the paperwork, and even found a carpenter to build our home. Strangely enough, she found a guy who wanted to do this for my family for a cheaper price. For most of my life I hadn't been a big believer in God, but I know now that things do· happen for a reason; the carpenter happened to be a distant cousin named Steave Sipe. It was very cool to see providence at work! Steave took care of the blueprints and everything. He would come down to Penn Brook and let me pick out the colors of the cabinets, countertops, and of course the carpets. Within three months the new home was built.

As I mentioned at the beginning of this chapter, the new house was really great for me and my family. A couple of weeks after we moved in, I purchased a van with wheelchair access so that I could go anywhere I wanted and have fun with my children. No more depending on county transportation, which came with a lot of rules and stipulations, and if you didn't follow them the van would not pick you up. It was a real pain in the butt.

Remember when I mentioned my son's accident? I said that when he came home from the hospital, he wasn't the same. What I meant is that, as I indicated earlier, we started having a lot of problems with him, both in school and at home. He had trouble controlling his anger, and he fell in with some other kids who were troublemakers. Remember I mentioned all of Dalton's different medications? I thought his drug use was under control and medically prescribed, but it turned out that it wasn't. These kids took advantage of him because of his brain injury. They had him drinking alcohol and doing drugs. He got into a lot of trouble. My mother and I could not control him, and he ended up getting locked up. It was very hard to visit him in jail, and painful when it was time to leave after each visit, but his incarceration did him a lot of good. I could even see it starting to change him. About a year later, he got to come home, for which everyone was happy and thankful.

As for my little girl, Chelsey, she really liked it in the new house and at her new school, even though she missed her friends and other things down in Penn Brook, such as her old school. As the years went by, I watched her growing up. She is a very intelligent girl. Her mother would be really proud, and I know I am. She also helps me a lot. I really love her and my son.

One day I got an unexpected visitor. It was a real shock to see who it was. Remember my friend Jimmy? I have already mentioned how we used to do everything together and how we became very close. After all these years, he finally came around to see me. It had always bothered me because I had not seen him and he was not there at all for me. But that didn't matter, I was just happy to see him. We talked a lot about the past, and inevitably I raised the issue of how he hadn't been around after my accident. He said it was because he didn't want to see me this way. Instead of lashing out with anger, I accepted this excuse like a man. But I thought to myself, *If this shit had happened to him, I would have been there for him and his family. Just like me and Tasha had always been.* A couple of hours later, Jimmy had to leave, but he told me that he would talk to me later and would be around more often. But guess what? He never came around again. So to me he isn't a friend.

CHAPTER SIX

MY OTHER FAMILY

One year after moving into our new home, my brother Lee met a woman named Tandy, who lived close by with her two kids, Zach and Ashley. My brother had three kids of his own – Billy, Lorry, and Emily. Billy and I were close when he was growing up. He is all grown up now but he visits us a lot, and we still have a lot of fun hanging out and talking about his childhood. He has a half-brother, Stevie, whom the whole family treats as if he were our own blood. As for Lorry, she comes around when she can. She is also all grown up and is about to have a baby. I wish her the best of luck. Lee and Emily's mom didn't last long, and the family does not speak to her since the separation because of her evil ways. She does not let us see Emily, but Lee sometimes sees her and gets pictures of her to show us. I hope that one day we can actually meet her.

After a few years of dating, Lee and Tandy were married. I was happy for him because he was one I had never thought would settle down. He was always dating one woman or another but something would eventually happen between them to end the relationship. Before my accident, Lee and I raised a lot of hell.

Mary, my other sister, lived in Camp Hill on the other side of the river from where we lived. It was not that far from us. She had three kids of her own – Pauline, Mardey, and Robert. She has been with a man named Bob ever since I was twelve. They have been together about twenty years now, which is hard to believe. Bob is an okay guy, but just like anyone else he has his problems. Mary's kids are pretty good, and I love them. My sister Minnie moved into an apartment close to us with her kids. My nephew Randy had some problems growing up, but he finally took on some responsibility. He started working, and now he is doing well. Even Brandy started working. So I am proud of them both.

As for my other niece and nephew, Rita and Paul, Rita moved to Arkansas and met a guy there and had two children with him, little Zan and Zin Anderson. They are really cool kids and Rita is turning out to be a good mother. I love them and I am also very proud of her. My nephew Paul got into some trouble and had to do some time in prison. I hope that when he gets out he will do better. Paul was the closest to me because we practically grew up together. I was only ten years old when Minnie gave birth to him. I really love that boy, too. I hope he gets his head straight and stays out of trouble.

My nieces and nephews have always been close to me. I used to babysit them all the time. One time my mother was babysitting them and my niece Rita did something wrong, so she climbed up a tree and would not come down until I got there. I tried to talk her into getting down, but she wouldn't listen to me either. So I ended up climbing up the tree to get her, and we sat up there for at least an hour. Eventually we both climbed down, but all that talking and bonding up in the tree drew us even closer.

My nephew Randy remembers riding on my dirt bike with me when he was young, and me taking him fishing. He was only four years old, and at the spot where we fished I had to watch him closely, because it was on a side of a bank with a four-foot drop to the water. I had to be very careful to make sure he did not fall in. Among my supplies, I had a tackle box. One time, I needed a new sinker for my fishing line, and Randy said something I will never forget. Instead of saying sinker he said, "Gunk gunk," imitating the sound. It was funny. Every time I went fishing afterward I would say that. Brandy and Paul remember good times as well, like when we would all wrestle and play games together. So as you can tell, the kids were all close to me growing up and they still are as teenagers and adults, which means a lot to me.

Something else good happened to me – one of my old friends, a woman named Sue, found out where I was living in my new house. I met Sue and her husband Rodney when Tasha and I got our first apartment. Sue had two kids, Cody and Russell. Cody would wait to eat dinner until I got home from work. They both got pretty close to me, just like my siblings and nieces and nephews. I have always been good with kids. A couple of years later, Sue and Rodney got a divorce, and right after that Tasha and I got into our accident. I didn't see any of them for a while until my family and I got our new house, but we were always very close. Sue was a very good friend and she still is to this very day.

I have talked to Rodney on and off since Penn Brook. He started coming to the house and we would drink a couple of beers and talk about the past. He had a brother named Larry who I met first through Jimmy. Larry was pretty cool; he and I also did a lot of drinking and fishing in the past. He still comes around from time to time, and we just talk a lot about stupid things we used to do. He always tells the story about me jumping off the bridge, and say how crazy I was. Another story he likes to tell is about me surfing on cars (you climb out of a moving car and onto the hood and stand up as if you were surfing, then you just climb back in). Looking back at that now, it was stupid. And I hope to God my son never tries that, or anyone else for that matter.

My other friend, George, also comes around often. He and I will always be close. He got married and has four kids of his own, three boys and one girl. I remember his first son very well. He was born shortly after my son, Dalton. George was very proud of him and that changed him too. As I mentioned earlier, having kids does change your personality for the better. And it makes you grow up. George and his family come up for cookouts and just to hang out with me and my kids. I am really glad we are still close. As for my friend Macho, I see him every now and then. He is not a people person; he likes to keep to himself, which I think can be a good thing. I learned that from him. Macho taught me a lot of things. I remember us hanging out in Harrisburg – he would show and tell me things about people and teach me what to do if I found myself in certain situations. Basically common sense.

As for me, I had to get new therapists, and that was a change for me. The sad thing is that I had to replace my favorite one, George Warner, because he retired. The good thing is that George and I are still in contact and he visits us as much as possible. He even got my daughter, Chelsey, into gymnastics. That was very cool of him; we even got to go down and watch her. And let me tell you, that was something – seeing all those little kids flipping around; it seemed like a kung-fu movie. It was fun and awesome to watch, and I was proud of her.

CHAPTER SEVEN

LIFE GOES ON

One evening I was chilling in bed watching TV about Tasha's and my favorite football team, the Washington Redskins. That made me think back to when I first started liking football. I have been a fan since 1990. About a year later, the Redskins won the Super Bowl. Since then I have been a big fan. Tasha was already a fan when I met her. At this time, my favorite players are Santana Moss and Clint Portis. My son is also a Redskins fan, but my nephew Randy is a Cowboys fan. And if you know football, you know the Redskins and the Cowboys despise each other. So we all watch football every Sunday. We argue with each other the entire time, then we eat together. It may sound kind of boring to others, but it feels good to share this connection of football with my family. As for Chelsey, I don't know where she went wrong but she likes the Steelers. As you can tell, I don't like them, but I have to give them credit for all the Super Bowls they have won. But one day the Redskins will be back in the Super Bowl – I know it.

One day, when my brother Lee and sister Minnie came to visit, we got to talking about the past. The conversation was about the bars, and I mentioned that I couldn't believe that I hadn't been to the bar since the accident. My brother and sister said, "Well let's go." I was all for it. After all, I did have my own transportation and nothing could stop us, so we went. I had such a good time going to the bar. It felt so normal.

I started going out more – with my sister's friend Dave, I went to a strip club for the first time in my life. It was on my birthday, and I was kind of nervous, but it was cool. I started to blend in like everyone else. After the club we went to a bar and had a few drinks. I consider Dave a friend. I needed a ramp built so that I could access my basement, and it needed to be built outside because the upstairs steps are too narrow; I would need an elevator and that would be a pain in the butt because I would need to transfer from my chair into it. That would take too much time, so I thought if I had a ramp outside I could get into my basement much more quickly and easily. Dave said he could build me one, and he gave me an idea of what it would look like. I liked his idea. So he drew up the blueprints and we got a permit to build it. Dave had one of his friends helping him with the work, and they completed it within two to three weeks – and that included dealing with bad weather.

When it was done, I went down into the basement, which had been completed at the same time as the rest of the house. When I entered, it seemed like another house entirely. It was nice, and it was different from upstairs. I had never been down there before, and although I had been told how it looked, accomplishing the feat of going downstairs myself was another thing entirely. I saw, out the comer of my eye, tears in Dave's eyes and in my mother's. Even I felt sad. But most of all I felt happy, because I could now access my entire house.

A couple of weeks after the ramp was built, I had a problem going to the bathroom. As I mentioned earlier, I have a catheter which relieves my bladder and which a nurse comes every month to change. One time, the morning after the nurse came to replace it, when I woke up my mother had to turn me on my side because I was hurting, and when she did so found that I was wet. Right away we knew something wasn't right, of course. She turned me on my back again so that we could call the nurse, and my catheter popped out. We did not panic because we had dealt with similar situations before. My mother called the office of the home care nurses and spoke to the supervisor, who said she would call the nurse responsible, and we had to wait until she called us back. And let me tell you, the wait was very, very painful. To understand what it felt like, just imagine you need to go to the bathroom but you can't at all. Also keep in mind that I couldn't move, so it's not as if I could walk around and shake the pain off. There was nothing to distract me from my increasing discomfort.

We waited for about twenty minutes without a call from the nurse, so we called the office for a second time and got the same story. The supervisor said she would call the nurse and we had to wait. What this meant was that I had to lay there in my bed and suffer. More time went by, and we called for a third time; this time, my mom was told that we had to call an ambulance. I thought to myself, *Oh great! Now it's going to take a lot more time.* When the EMTs arrived, I had to go through for their benefit the whole story of what had happened. They also had to call the nurse's office to get the story of why she couldn't come out. While they were asking me questions, I was in so much pain that I was nearly in tears, and I couldn't talk very well because I was hurting so badly. I got so mad that I starting yelling and cursing, as I think anyone would have in my place. Finally the EMTs took me to the hospital – and guess what? I had to lie there for hours! I overheard the nurses talking about my catheter, and would you believe they said they hadn't changed my kind of catheter since medical school? The difference in catheters is that mine goes straight into my bladder while most others reach the bladder through the urethra. So I had to wait some more, until finally the hospital staff got hold of Dr. Owens. He explained to them how to change my type of catheter. They put a new one in successfully. I felt very relieved that it was working. I had to wait until the EMS workers showed up to take me home, but the worst was over. My mom did call the nurse's office and put in a complaint about everything that had happened.

I want to say one last thing about this incident. The nurse who first came to change my catheter was very competent, and by no means was the procedure hurtful. I think the hospitals and other medical treatment facilities are understaffed. It's my opinion that unfortunate situations like the one I endured happen because the nurses in the field are overworked, and there are too few of them to handle everything. Regardless, I am just trying to get my readers to realize what it's like to live with a disability. You have your good days and your bad days. I hope this book will help people know what to do if something happens to a family member or a friend. If you take nothing else away from this book, remember this: Even if someone becomes paralyzed in an accident or is born with a disability, they can still live a good life.

CHAPTER EIGHT

MEETING NEW PEOPLE

Meeting new people for the first time is kind of weird, because you don't yet know what kind of personality they have or whether they will accept you for who you are. My sister Minnie met a guy named Tommy and they got together. I like him, he has a cool personality, and I am happy for her. Tommy has some cool friends; his one buddy's wife, Angie, is a strong person because she been through hell herself, having battled cancer, which is an awful disease to live and deal with. I hope embryonic stem cells can help cure or reverse the effects of cancer as well. From what I have read and heard, stem cells could potentially help with a lot of different disabilities and diseases. Anyone who can fight cancer is a very strong person in my book. My uncle Bobby found out late in life that he had cancer, even though he had quit smoking many years before. He had been in the U.S. Navy in the 1940s. Back then, the ships were not very safe inside, medically speaking. It takes years for the kind of cancer he had to develop. By the time he was diagnosed, it was too late, and Uncle Bobby died. He was a very good man, and it is for the sake of other good men and women like him that I hope they find a cure for cancer, as well as for many other diseases and disabilities. His death was hard to deal with for everyone in the family, especially Aunt Josie and his kids. So when you're feeling sorry for yourself and helpless, just remember there is always someone out there in a worse situation. That's how I look at life's trials and deal with them.

I want to mention the fact that my sister Minnie and my mom are my home healthcare nurses. The nurses I had in the past did not work out. The first nurse had to quit because of health issues, and I found out that the second one was stealing from me. I first began to suspect during a trip to the mall; I tried to make a purchase but was short on money, and I knew I had had more than what was there. I might be paralyzed, but I am not stupid. One day I made sure to mention in front of the nurse that I had eighty dollars in my lockbox, which I knew wasn't hard to open. Later that day, I went outside while she remained in my bedroom. When she left for the day, I asked my mom to check the box, and just as I expected half of it was missing. My mom, the nurse, and I had been the only ones at home the whole day. So I called. UCP and told them that I didn't want her working for me anymore. I didn't give the true reason; I just told the office that we weren't getting along. Even though she had done me wrong, I didn't want her to get arrested; she had a little son of her own to care for. Nevertheless, it really hurt my family to know what she had done, because we had treated her with respect, and she had been like family.

The nurse I got after the one who stole from me was pretty cool, and she worked with me for over four years, until one day she had to quit for personal reasons. That was pretty sad, but I am used to saying goodbye to nurses after growing close to them. This time, it led to a great turn of events. UCP left my mom and sister to be my nurses, which is good for many reasons. The main reason is that I don't have to watch them all the time. I trust my family with my life. After all, if it wasn't for them – especially my mother – my kids and I would not be here right now.

I am fortunate to have a family like that. One thing I found out quickly in the nursing home is that not everyone has family there for them. My friend Buzz was one of those unfortunate people. He did have family, but his mother was up in age and his kids had a lot of responsibility of their own. One day, I was downstairs in my house and my mother came downstairs to tell me she had read in the newspaper that Buzz had passed away. I felt very bad because the last time I had seen him we had made plans to hang out at the nursing home. His passing was very hard for me, but I pray for him every night as well as for my family members who have died. Especially my Tasha. I talk to her every night.

Minnie's boyfriend Tommy, whom I have already mentioned, has become a pretty good friend of mine. I try to go over to his house at least every other weekend. We sit around drinking a few beers and just talking and listening to music. He is a good man and I am glad my sister found him. They are made for each other. Once a year, Tommy has a game feast at which he serves dishes of the various game animals he and his friends have hunted. I will not eat anything like that, but I like going just for the beer and the opportunity to meet new people. Some of his friends I like very much – I have already mentioned Angie and her husband Bobby. Bill and Dexter are two others. Bill has a personality like mine and Tommy's. When I first met him we drank some beer and talked a lot about life and kids. Tommy was there for Dexter growing up. He took him hunting and fishing and other cool stuff like that. Dexter is younger than me, but we can hold a conversation. He is a good kid. He would do anything for anyone; he's just that type of person. Years ago, I thought I would never talk to or meet people again, but I am living proof that you can still have a life after becoming disabled. It just takes time to realize after a terrible accident.

I wish that everyone who needed home healthcare nurses could be cared for by family members. If that is not possible for you, make sure you meet and find out more about the nurse before she is hired to take care of you. I wish there had been someone to give me that advice years ago, even though I probably would have not listened. Keep in mind that dealing with a stranger as your nurse can be a pain in the ass in the long run. Thank God for Mom and Sis. With them I have no doubts, and I don't have to worry about my stuff going missing.

CHAPTER NINE

NEW THERAPISTS AND OTHER THINGS IN LIFE

I have mentioned my former therapist George and the fact that he had to retire, although he still comes around to see me and is like part of the family now. UCP found me new therapists to work with, though it took some time to get used to them. But as the years went by, I learned a lot of patience. They did a good job with me, keeping me loose and limber and keeping my blood circulating. Maintaining proper circulation is very important when you are in my situation.

It's also important to drink a lot of water to prevent yourself from getting bladder infections. I know some people think water tastes bad, and I thought the same thing back when I used to drink a lot of Gatorade and other sugary drinks. I never had a taste for water.

But if you suffer a terrible accident like I did, you will need to do a lot of things afterward that you never would have done before. A lot of things change. And drinking water is a lot better than infections, trust me.

I also had to become accustomed to lying on my side instead of my back to prevent bed sores. It took me years to realize the importance of these precautions. I hope this information helps someone in my situation to save a lot of time and suffering.

My family and I have been in our new home for six years now, and I recently got a new wheelchair. In the course of those few years, technology has changed a lot. My new wheelchair has a lot more power than the old one, and it seems as if it has four-wheel drive. I can go over bumps now that I couldn't before, and I have a greater sense of freedom and control.

Speaking of technology, I am getting pretty good on my computer. They came out with a newer version of Dragon Dictate that understands my voice very well. It's fairly easy to use, you just need to learn your commands and learn Alpha Bravo, and that's all you need to spell words. Or if you want the program to write the words you say, rather than writing one letter at a time, just say, "Dictate Mode," and it will switch to that mode. As for using a mouse, all you have to do is say, "Mouse Grid," and nine big squares show up on the screen. To move the mouse, you just choose the block closest to where you want to navigate on the screen. You get used to it pretty quickly, it just takes some practice. Dictation programs truly are worth all the time it takes to learn them. To be able to operate the computer on your own is priceless. I am using Dragon Dictate to write this book, though with the help of my daughter Chelsey. There are some things I just can't do with the program, so having Chelsey help me saves a lot of time. It is our way to bond and spend time together.

I love my kids; they mean everything to me. If it wasn't for them, I wouldn't know what to do. My son Dalton is in a pretty cool school now. I like the way the teachers treat the kids and how they handle them. Their treatment plans are different from most other schools. One of Dalton's classes is martial arts, which I think is great for the kids. Most of them are at this alternative school because of anger issues, and martial arts helps to relieve a lot of their anger and also gives them a positive outlet for anger, so that it won't be directed inappropriately at others. It helps with their attitude towards other people as well. I hope to see my son upgrade to another belt within a week. I will be going down to the school to watch his test, and I can't wait. I think it's going to be very cool. My son is almost sixteen now, and my daughter is almost fourteen. WOW! That makes me feel really old. It has been thirteen years since my accident, though it still seems like only yesterday. Thinking back, I know

I have learned a lot since then and have been through so much. But I am still here and so is my family.

Since I'm discussing technology and other new things in my life, I need to mention that I just recently got over another bed sore. It didn't take anywhere near the time to heal that the previous one did. The visiting nurses got me a machine called a Wound VAC. The acronym stands for vacuum assisted closure; it's a machine that sucks all the fluid out of your sore and at the same time slowly shrinks the wound. But you still need to lie flat and on your sides as much as possible to speed the healing process. If you find yourself dealing with a bed sore, try not to sit up if you don't have to – trust me, the sore will heal, and avoiding certain positions and motions will save you a lot of time. You might not think so at first, but just keep doing what you normally do for a sore, which is to clean it every day, and otherwise try to go on with everyday living, though if you aren't careful certain normal behaviors can make it even worse. So if you ever have that problem, remember the Wound VAC and give it a try. It will work.

I hope future technology and cures, especially those promised by embryonic stem cells, can help all of us. I believe stem cells will work for multiple reasons. I know from what I have read that they can help in the treatment of cancer, tumors, Alzheimer's, and disabilities resulting in a loss of motor function or mobility. In other words, they could help a friend or relative walk again. My aunt Rachel is currently dealing with a brain tumor. I hope to God that she overcomes it. She is a great person and will help anyone in need. I just don't want to see her fail at fighting this disease when I know we can cure it. I am proud of Obama, our new president. He has approved embryonic stem cell research, and I think that is awesome. We are finally on the right track. The United States is one of the richest countries in the world but one of the only ones that did not allow embryonic stem cell research. Finally, thanks to an executive order issued by President Obama that has changed.

At this present time, our economy is in desperate need of recovery. There are many foreclosures on homes and a lot of people struggling just to live their everyday lives. I think our country should try some new and strange things to help our economy. Certain people approve of gambling, which the government already allows, and taxes. Another thing that the government should legalize and tax is marijuana. I'm not one for drugs, but I believe marijuana helps a lot of people with chronic pain and those in situations like mine, as well as people with cancer and other diseases and disabilities. You never hear of anyone overdosing on it or getting into fights over it. I believe, and so do others, that the legalization of marijuana could help us with everyday life and also help the economy. I know a lot of people might not agree with this idea, and everyone has the right to disagree. After all, this is the home of the free. But we do need to start thinking of the future – for ourselves, our children, and our children's children.

We also need to do something about this war in Iraq. It has been going on for years now, and we are losing a lot of young men and women. I agree with the reason that we went to war in Afghanistan, for what the terrorists did to us by running our own planes into the World Trade Center and the Pentagon. But I think we should have gone into Iraq with a better plan, if we went in at all. Once there, we should have taken care of business quickly, and then focused more on catching Bin Laden. After all, he was the main terrorist behind the assault on our homeland.

Now I am hearing about Iran, as if an invasion of that country might be coming soon. We don't need another war right now; we are spending too much already. We cannot afford another war. I hope our president does everything he can to avoid that, but at the same time, he has to keep us safe. He has a hell of a job, and I would not want that burden. Some people think they could do a better job than him, but they need to stop and think about what they are wishing for. I am only adding my input about the economy and the war because it has a lot to do with our lives. And I can't help but think that if we didn't have to spend all this money on war, we would have more funds for stem cell research and a lot of other things, such as more jobs for the disabled and those in need.

Since my accident, I have tried many different jobs, but none have succeeded. I tried jobs on the Internet and lost a lot of money. I also tried to start a painting business with a few employees. I purchased a van and all the equipment for the business. I did manage to get a few clients, but it was just too hard to keep track of all the workers and make sure they did their jobs right. What I soon realized is that I needed a person I could trust to make sure everyone had gotten their jobs done. With nobody to watch over my employees while they worked, some of the work was not done the way it should have been. The business cost me some money before I realized this, but it wasn't too bad; it was just enough to make me realize the business would cost a lot more in the long run. So after my last job, I shut down the business and sold everything I had purchased for it. I know I did not succeed, but at least I tried, which is more than what some people do. I know guys who are able to walk and are capable of working who do nothing but sit around on their asses and live off other people. Laziness is something that I can't stand, and it is very sad to see. If I can still try to work despite my disability, why can't they?

I would like to mention a topic I never thought I would talk about, and that is finding love again. I haven't yet found it, but I want everyone to know that just because you are paralyzed it doesn't mean your love life is over. Over the years I have had a few female friends with whom I have shared intimate moments. After the accident, I thought my sex life was over, and sex is something you don't want to give up because it really makes you feel alive inside. You may not be able to do certain things that you could in the past, such as making love. You just have to improvise, and go with what you have. After my accident, I hooked up with one old female friend with whom I have always had chemistry, but never had the chance to explore a relationship because I was in love with my Tasha and my friend had someone in her life as well. But now those reasons are gone. We still talk to this very day about having a relationship, but something keeps preventing it from getting off the ground. Even if we don't accomplish a relationship, we will always be friends. If I don't find romantic love in my life again, that's okay. I have my kids – and that's enough love for a lifetime.

CHAPTER TEN

BE STRONG, KEEP FIGHTING, THERE'S HOPE

I decided to write this book to express my feelings and thoughts about living with disabilities. It isn't healthy never to speak about a traumatic event, and I was aware that I needed to talk about my accident and my current condition. But I have never felt comfortable talking to anyone, so expressing my feelings in this book has been good for me, and my hope is that it can help someone else in a similar situation.

When I came home from the nursing home, I was happy to be with my family. But through it all I felt empty inside. I didn't let anyone know of my feelings, however, because I felt that I deserved to suffer as a result of what had happened. I still feel that way sometimes, and though over time this guilt has become easier to deal with, it will never go away entirely. Like most victims of trauma, I have learned to accept it. I am lucky to have my family here for me. If it wasn't for them, I don't know how I would have made it through life since the accident. Everyone should have a person they can trust and depend on. For many of us that's not always possible, but we just have to do the best we can and live on.

As I said earlier, I got new therapists, and they worked with me very well. I never regained the full use of my arms, but I can move my shoulders and my right arm and I can pick up and swing my arm in and out. That comes in handy because on my wheelchair I need to hit a toggle switch in order to drive in reverse. I am also getting more feeling back in my legs. It isn't much, but it is something to be excited about; it makes exercising much easier and gives me more confidence. Even though I never regained a lot of movement during therapy, my therapists still worked with me to keep what movement I did have and to strengthen my muscles. My occupational therapist (OT) worked with my arms, putting them through a range of motion and also on occasion hooking me up to a machine that would shock my arms to stimulate the nerves and hopefully recover more movement. I could feel different parts of my arm jumping. It wasn't painful; it was really cool to see parts of my body moving that hadn't moved in a long time. My physical therapist (PT) worked on my legs. She also put me through a lot of range of motion exercises, which are important for those with disabilities so that they can stay limber and keep their blood flowing. I get into my stander every week, which helps my blood to flow and also puts pressure on my feet. I really like standing – I had dreamed of regaining the ability to stand ever since waking up from my coma. I thought I would never stand again, but thanks to technology I can. A stander is a chair which you get into and to which you then attach the front and back pieces that keep your knees from buckling. It has a lever that you move to make the chair stand up – after a few times of pushing the lever back and forth, you start to stand. And that's how it works. It feels really good after my workout, I can actually feel the difference in my body. It kind of feels as if I have been stretched – that is the best way I can explain it. So I continue my workouts and the range of motion exercises every week. That's what I do to stay in shape, hoping the day will come when embryonic stem cells will allow me to recover more of my former abilities. And I hope this book will inspire its readers to keep fighting, even when a tragedy strikes.

At the end of 2009 something great happened! My kids got in contact with their brother, Brandon, they started talking, and the renewal of this relationship led to them meeting Sharon, Tasha's mom, their other grandmother. I talked to Brandon myself, and something he said took a lot off my chest. Brandon said, "I do not blame you for the accident." The issue of how he felt toward me had been on my mind for years. I am so happy the kids have reunited with Brandon and their other family. This is like a dream come true, and I hope everything continues to go well.

It has been years since my accident, and I am still learning to accept my disability. But I am learning to live again.

To my mother,

thank you for always being there.

I love you

BONUS CHAPTER 1

It's been some time since I had my book published. The publishing company that I had. Went out of business, so I thought I would add some more to my story. The last couple years I lost some family members first my niece Rita, Aunt Martha, my cousin Erica, and the worst of all my son. That tour me up inside I lost all feelings inside and all beliefs. Once you read my book you will see the trouble my son was heading for. The people he was hanging with was no good. They were into heroin one of the worst drugs you can get hooked on, and they use it the worst way with a needle.

Once I knew I did all I could to stop him, I tried to help the law catch the people who were dealing the drug. I told them who they were, but they did not do anything to catch them they just let it go until it was too late for my son. The county I live in new my son since he was 10 years old, he got into a lot of trouble, especially in school. But as he got older the trouble got worse, he was put on probation and of course he did not listen. So they sent him to prison, where I think it really went wrong.

He had his court hearing and they sent him to a rehab where he could get help. I thought that would help him but I did not know it was for alcohol not for the drug he was addicted to. They would let them go out 2 hours a day, and when they got back they would give them a breathalyzer test. Let me remind you my son was not and there for alcohol, not that terrible drug he was on. You got to test using a urine sample or blood test.

Not a breathalyzer test, then my son got into a fight instead of calling his probation officer or the cops they kicked him out the rehab. He was there on a court order he was not allowed to leave and of course he took off and went to some friend's house. That's where he started using again, a couple days after he left the rehab my son overdose and passed away. I was watching my favorite football team on TV the Washington Redskins when this number came on my TV it was the Harrisburg corner my heart dropped. They'd told us my son has overdosed, the friend's house he was at said they found him like that when they got up.

I think they should take their time and look at the charges before they sentence these young kids, and look at all the different rehabs. The thing that really bothers me is, they caught my son with the drugs on him when he overdosed before. After he recovered the police had a talk with him about the drugs on him, and where he got them from. He would not say anything, my son would not snitch on no one. I think they should let the kids recover and then asked questions, but before they ask. They should give them 2 chores either go to a rehab of our chores, or go to prison. But they don't do that, and instead they try to make them snitch and everyone will know what they did so they got to live in fear all of their life. That puts a lot on the person, so instead that pushes them right back into using I know there got to be a better option than making the kids tell snitch.

I hope they make better decisions than what they did with my son, so no parent or loved one goes through the heartbreak I did. My daughter is doing the same thing I don't want to lose another kid, she needs to get herself together and make a better life. I will do what I can, but she needs to make an effort.

Losing my son took everything out of me I know it hurt a lot of people and family but he was more than just my son he was my best friend. Another person that took it real hard, was my mother Pauline.

She was really close to my son, since the accident she is the one that's always been there for my kids and me. I'm so lucky to have a mother like that if it was not for her me and my kids would not be here.

My mother is the one that took care of everything, the funeral and all of the arrangements. My son wanted to be cremated, so his ashes sit beside me on a desk.

Just the author day, I searched my daughter's room and found some things I wish I did not find. So what I did I feel ashamed of, I had to snitch on my baby girl I called her probation officer and told them what I found, and told him they better come and search her bedroom or I a.m. going to sue you are content the news.

I told them, I will not lose another kid. We went through the same thing with my son, they played around until it was too late for him. They came and search her room within a couple hours, and they found a lot more.

So they took my daughter to jail, and they are talking about a rehab I will make sure it is a good one.

I finally got her in a place where I can help her!

That is all I know so far about her arrangements, they are going to give her a choice prison on rehab.

If she chooses rehab they are going to make a plan for her. That's good, as long as I see it before they make a choice.

I am going to try and sell my house, so we can have a new start in life. Maybe before my daughter comes home that would be great in my grandson can make some good new memories for all of us.

Not long ago I had to get a new Van, I thought I was not going to have one because of all the things: that went wrong. But with the help of my nurse and other people we were able to purchase a van and they approve me, the funds to have it adapted for me. The funds were more than what I paid for the van, so I a.m. thankful for all the help I received from everyone. From all the things I've been through with losing my son and trying to get my daughter on the right track. It's about time something went right now we can get away and have some fun for wants. My grandson likes Cowboys and animals so I like taking him to the zoo and other places. This Christmas 2017 we got my grandson a rocking horse and other things Cowboys have and where. He loves that damn rocking horse, it makes all kinds of different noises.

I don't care about the noise, just so he's happy. I want to spend much time with him as I can't, don't know how long I will be here. Before I join my son and other loved ones. I can't wait until then but before I do leave this world, I will spend my time loving my grandson darter mother and other loved ones.

It's been 20 years since the accident and I know my time is running out its coming one day, but not yet. Until then I still hope my book can help someone in my shape or anyone in general. To hang in there and keep fighting no matter what. Don't give up someone needs you may be a love one or even yourself.

It's better to go out with a fight then just to give up. My mother has went through a lot in her life and she is steel fighting. I guess, that's where I get my strength from, and the wheel to not give up. My mother is the most loving, strongest woman I know. Everyone in our family comes to me are mom for help, that's just the way are family is. We always been a close family, that's all we had coming up in the city. There was no one we could deep end on, we just had each other.

When we lost my niece Rita, it devastated everyone in the family. It was on Valentine's Day around 2012 we got the call, it was my other niece Pauline telling us we better call about Rita, she heard something on the news, and it did not sound good. Before we could call, my sister came over and told us her daughter got shot over stupid drugs. My sister Minnie her mom came over that morning, and she was really upset. We could not believe what had happened, she was just here on vacation. I took her and her two kids, to chalky cheese. We had a real good time. After we got the call we checked the news to find out what happened, they said she was shot point-blank in the head. My girl did not deserve that, she was a great mom, just got caught up with the wrong people. Then just as we thought we heard everything, my niece's kids were up stairs from where it had been. Her 2 sons, seen their mom laying on the floor, not moving.

The worst of all, it was her nephew from her dad's first marriage. He was high on drugs, and wanted money and was too lazy to work. He lived off of my niece!

So after hearing that, and finding out the young Dick head just got eight years. Her 2 sons got to grow up with no mother. People are so lucky I cannot walk, because a lot of people would pay.

There are a couple more loved ones I lost. My aunt Martha was another close member of my family that I was close to. She was more than an aunt to me, she was more like a grandmother to me.

We lost her about one year before my son, that lady went through hell every day also. She had to go to dialysis three times a week, but she hung in there for a long time. I do not know how she done that week after week, and she done that over 10 years. I know people that done dialysis for one week, and that person died. So it's not easy!

Another person that took it hard was my mother Pauline, who was my Aunt Martha sister they were real close. They had it rough growing up together, so did their other siblings.

Not long after my cousin Erica died, she was also murdered. It was over drugs to. The guy that murdered

Erica, took her car. After murdering her, he took her body and dropped it off in the words. We did not know where she was, they looked everywhere even my house, her job, and other family homes and friends' houses.

Finally they found her not to far from my house back in the woods, she was laying there over a week.

They did catch him, and they gave him life in person.

BONUS CHAPTER 2

The only thing keeping me going is my grandson, my son's baby's mom Melissa brings my grandson over t to our house every other weekend, and holidays to see us.

We take him all over, the mall is his favorite just like his father. That's where I took my kids shopping. I promise my son I will do anything I can for his son, and to leave him something for his future now and when I die. I will make sure he got something for his future, all I want is for my grandson to do good in life. That's all I wanted for my kids, and I tried to do everything I could.

I will keep providing for my grandson, and I will do everything I can for my darter Chelsea.

My mother and I, will try and help Chelsea break away from her addiction. It will be a long road to travel, but we will get there, we always do. She needs a good rehab, and I need to find one because her PO said insurance will only pay for one month. She needs a lot more than that!

Our family been through this before with my son, so I don't want to make the same mistakes I made with him. Such as not paying attention to what's going on, and trying not to believe what's happening. There is a lot of things I could have done better, but they need to admit they have a problem before we can help them.

We need to find out a way to fix this drug addiction, we have in our country. So we don't keep losing our love ones. There got to be a way we can all pull together and help these kids.

I was thinking to myself, it all comes down to money like all things do. But they need to make a life changing choice, either give up on drugs are else face person time, or you can go to a good rehab and start rebuilding your life. Once they make the good choice of rehab, then issue a credit card of sort.

So they can make a fresh start, like paying off their fines and costs. That way they can start working and pay off the credit card. At the same time they're paying off some of the mistakes and bad choices they made. I think that would give them some responsibility, and respect they need to get back to reality.

That's what I think, but there is always a better way just someone needs to pull the trigger and get moving on this issue.

I will like to talk about my uncle Bobby and his family, I wrote about them in my book. They help me and my family through the accident and after. A couple years ago we lost Uncle Bobby, he was a great man.

He would do anything to help someone out, especially kids. Uncle Bobby and his wife Josie they would take candy and toys to the local hospital, every holiday. That's the kind of people we need more in this world. I want to say thank you a lot Uncle Bobby may you rest in peace.

Sadly to say his darter has cancer my cousin Deb, she does a lot for my family also. She loved my son

Dalton, she took his death hard to. Everyone did, I am like. Just trying to give you a picture of how she was to my son. I just hope she makes it through this cancer, she got a lot of love to give.

Deb I want you to know I love you and thank you for your love and help you gave, me and my family.

I don't want this book to sound all terrible, there is some good. Like my grandson, I have a new nurse, and also her husband James. We are close, when he comes up with his wife Lindsay to work, we have a lot of fun. Even if it's just to hang out, watch TV play games are just have a good laugh.

But he and Lindsay, help me and mom a lot. Like work around the house, cleaning up outside, such as cutting the grass, trimming brushes and other things we need done. Also they have two kids together

Isaiah and Layla they are good kids. They even do what they can to help, and my grandson likes them also.

When he comes over for his visit, it works out for us. Because they keep him busy, and it's good for him to have other kids to play with. Not to say he is not around other kids, because his mother got him in day care.

That's one of the good things I can say about her, the young lady keeps a job and supports her son. Even though Melissa and my son did not work out, they made a beautiful young man.

One of the most talked about stories in Pennsylvania is marijuana. They are still against legalizing marijuana in our state. All they want is the money, they don't care about the people who could use it.

Even myself can benefit from it, but most important is these kids that really needs marijuana to live.

They are having these seizures, which it is very hard to watch. The medicine they give them to stop the seizures are not working. But it is proven marijuana helps, why keep forcing pills down there mouth.

They keep saying marijuana is a gateway drug, but it's not. Alcohol is the gateway drug, and that is in every grocery store and corner stores in America. It's all about money!

If it wasn't about the money, why in some states marijuana is legal, and not just for medical reasons. But because it helps for many other diseases, and injuries.

A couple friends of mine were talking about way back in the day when everything was legal. Until they started making new laws such as legalizing alcohol, and made marijuana illegal. It makes you think if they would have made marijuana legal instead of alcohol, I think and many others think, America would have been better off.

Before ending this book I want to dedicate it to a couple of people. I want to say, to my darter Chelsea all I wanted for you is to have a good life, and raise a beautiful family and just enjoy life take it one day at a time. I know you can! To my grandson I love you, and don't listen to the negative stories you hear about your father. Your dad had a hard life and that's my fault. I should have never got on my bike, but I did and that was the worst mistake I ever made. Your grand mal Tosha and I, was celebrating our birthdays, because they were a couple of days apart. We stopped at a friend's house to stay overnight, so we did not have to drink and drive. But something happened there, I got into a fight and they told me I need to leave.

So I did, I started heading towards my other friends house Rodney. It was not too far to travel, but before we could get there we were forced off the road. That's where our lives began the journey down the toilet.

It was not all bad, we had good times as a family, we did what we could with the cards we were dealt.

I wanted you to know D about your father and us meaning grand mal Chelsea, and I your grandfather.

It really seems like our family is cursed or something, but yet we still keep fighting. 20 years of fighting and losing loved ones, my time should be coming, but until then I will keep fighting and living my second chance.

CPSIA information can be obtained
at www.ICGtesting.com
Printed in the USA
BVHW030112220322
632066BV00020B/105